A
Night
FOR THE
LADY

OTHER BOOKS
BY JOANNE ARNOTT

Wiles of Girlhood (1991)

Ma MacDonald (1992)

My Grass Cradle (1993)

Breasting the Waves: On Writing & Healing (1995)

Steepy Mountain: Love Poetry (2004)

Mother Time: Poems New & Selected (2007)

Salish Seas: An Anthology of Text & Image, Editor (2011)

Chapbooks

Longing: Four Poems on Diverse Matters (2008)

The Family of Crow (2012)

A
Night
FOR THE
LADY

JOANNE ARNOTT

RONSDALE

A NIGHT FOR THE LADY
Copyright © 2013 Joanne Arnott

RONSDALE PRESS
3350 West 21st Avenue
Vancouver, B.C., Canada V6S 1G7
www.ronsdalepress.com

Typesetting: Julie Cochrane, in New Baskerville 11 pt on 13.5
Cover Design: Julie Cochrane
Cover Art: Aaron Paquette
Paper: Ancient Forest Friendly Rolland Opaque — 100% post-consumer
     waste, totally chlorine-free and acid-free

Ronsdale Press wishes to thank the following for their support of its publishing program: the Canada Council for the Arts, the Government of Canada through the Canada Book Fund, the British Columbia Arts Council, and the Province of British Columbia through the Book Publishing Tax Credit Program.

Library and Archives Canada Cataloguing in Publication

Arnott, Joanne, 1960–, author
   A night for the lady / Joanne Arnott.

Poems.
Issued in print and electronic formats.
ISBN 978-1-55380-250-1 (print)
ISBN 978-1-55380-251-8 (ebook) / ISBN 978-1-55380-252-5 (pdf)

   I. Title.

PS8551.R773N53 2013   C811'.54   C2013-903159-6   C2013-903160-X

At Ronsdale Press we are committed to protecting the environment. To this end we are working with Canopy (formerly Markets Initiative) and printers to phase out our use of paper produced from ancient forests. This book is one step towards that goal.

Printed in Canada by Marquis Book Printing, Quebec, Canada

CONTENTS

my poor bird

conflict zone

longing: five poems on diverse matters

—

experiment

—

floruit

—

ACKNOWLEDGEMENTS

Many storytellers, singers and poets have contributed to the making of this collection; some I have named and some I have not. These poems arising from conversations and engagements with the world would not have come to be without the strength, intelligence, sensitivity, sense of timing and evocative turns of phrase of many other people within my beautiful web of family and friends.

Special thanks to Lee Maracle, Russell Wallace and the many Aboriginal Writers Collective West Coast writers, and to Maria Campbell, and the many indigenous writer-mums who have influenced and inspired me through books and via the e-groups Old Lady Hunting and storytellersplayspace, and other gathering places. Thanks to Duncan Mercredi, Annharte, and all the AWC of Manitoba, and to Jamie Reid, John Barlow and Alastair Campbell, and all the riverspine-whalesnail-newrivertrain associated writers, for cross-mentoring and poetic play. More recently, thanks to Jim Wong-Chu and the Asian Canadian Writers Workshop fellow-travellers. Thanks again to my children for allowing me to quote them.

I must also give thanks to those who make it a life's work to translate classical Chinese, Japanese, Persian, Arabic, Aramaic, Sumerian, Sanskrit, Greek, Hebrew, Hindi, Salish, Inuit, Mohawk, Michif, French, Spanish, Irish, Scottish, Latin, and many other literatures — in particular the songs and the poetries, and the medical and spiritual treatises — so that I and many others may be nourished en route, with a wealth of old songs and traditional stories to help us make sense of our lives.

A number of the poems in this collection (or earlier versions of same) have previously been presented in the following journals: *CV2, Exile Quarterly, First Nations House Magazine, Front: Contemporary Art and Ideas, Rampike Magazine, Schroedinger's Cat, The New Chief Tongue, West Coast Line, Windsor Review, Vox Feminarum* and *Dublin Poetry Review's Heroes Congress 1.0*; as well as in the following collections and chapbooks: *Force Field, Alive at the Centre, Can You Hear Me Now: A Tribute to Jamie Reid, Other Tongues: Mixed Race Women Speak Out, Rock Salt: An Anthology of Contemporary BC Poetry, Longing: Four Poems on Diverse Matters*, and or created for and presented at these events: *Pickton Farm Rally for Hope* and *Strong Words: A Celebration of Aboriginal Poets of BC.*

my poor bird

watching the earth breathe

with thanks to Giles Slade, after Raymond Carver

watching the earth breathe
can become habit-forming, wind
touching incessantly at our clothes
tossing our hair, tousling spirits

we are water settling from sky
gathering in the folds of leaves
seeping into soil
watching the earth breathe

can become habit-forming
done tenderly with heart stirring
watching the earth newborn
on a grey morning. he told me

ideas travel first in drops
rills of thought become creeks
springs erupt into streams, streams into rivers
rivers open-mouthed to the sea

where thought comes together
with other thought
it pleases me

seahorse migrations

falling in love with our stories as
they rise from their deep-rooted places

called forth by
any little question
a chance encounter

an imagined look upon an imagined face, and all
remembered glimpses
of past times

drifting upward now —
quick & quick —
seeking the air
in droves

here the golden one
here the hungry one
here the singing one
this one, afraid

each tail has slipped its mooring as
sunlight calls through whispering water
urgent for redemption

craving the air &
all good things
that may happen there

deep plants remain and growing
seahorses ever hopeful

rise & rise

reflections (interdependence)

the three of us
sun & moon & earth
weave our webbed light

old moon held in young moon's arms
shining by the light of the ocean
& the inland sea

my poor bird
take thy flight

lift away into stardust & radiance
interplanetary messenger & escapee
defeating the demons at last

dream of fine houses

dream of fine houses grown organically and
walking the landscape on chicken legs, fine
stone grain or weathered board, skin over limb
for that distinctive bone-rack effect
o ownership
o ownership of the material elements of self
to toss down a dish-cloth and open a river
to throw down a fine-toothed comb
and unleash the eruption of forests
this horn on my head
plucked and posted by the gate
listening carefully to the animals
i slip between the dangers of the neighbourhood
i receive the gifts of the powerful baba
and live oh yes i live to tell the tale

poems poems poems

I used to live across the street from a strip joint
my eldest son & his friend mortified me to no end

after we'd stepped over the needles and condoms
all the way to kindergarten and/or the corner store

we would pause for the light to cross the street
and the pulsing music would cause these five-year-old boys

to dance! dance with elation! how
can i hold a sour look

given the hilarity
i am feeling

now my son is twenty-one
moving out this weekend with his king-size bed

i am building a poetry joint across the way
poems! poems! poems! on display

the poet thugs of Saskatoon

the poet thugs
of Saskatoon

remind the lone
Dene of past wars

we're good now
aren't we? they tease

the scrawny
young liberal

with his fold-over
posture

does not attend
the events

that might console
might empower him

he joins us
in the lounges

of Saskatoon
the lone Dene

baits the writers
one by one

insulting
slurring

soon he is spewing
hatred and contempt

for the Cree —

every single person
at the table knows

it is time for him to go
before he does

he clings to a woman
who shirks him off

the poet thugs escort him
to the hotel doors

the feminist-lesbians call
leave it to the men

our men
will handle it

the Dene flies
into a taxi

a Cree poet
tugs on the locked door

a Cree professor
reflects on his youth

and the movie
300

we are not Cree
he cries aloud

we are Spartans
damnit

a week later
six hundred kilometres further east

the scrawny young liberal
has become an eight-foot giant

teeth crack'd and arms tatoo'd
shank in his pocket

menacing visage worthy
of the time, attention, and stories

of the poet thugs
of Saskatoon

under the birches (black ponies)

when she was small, she befriended
a black pony she noticed
his teeth were very big
and very dirty
and so
as often
as she could
she slipped out
of the house with
her father's toothbrush
the pony loved her attentions
and her father never found out

then, when she was a young teen
she dated a man twice her age
when she finally got up
the power to effect
a break-up
she found
suddenly planted
like a fixture in the kitchen
every single day, the very man
who courted and lost the daughter
courted the father and won: she left
the house to him, and went to live with

the black ponies

constance

with thanks to Connie Fife

when i was pregnant, she told me
reaching back more than twenty years
for the memory

i put sunflower seeds on my belly
i used to read aloud to my son
so he could hear our bones

i love our voices, she said

some gifts are true, uprising
from the core of human being

these outweigh the lesser gifts

chickadee & sparrow flutter down
lured by the seeds and undisturbed
by our voices

i put your hand on my belly
i invite you to read this aloud
i want to listen to our bones

& to love our voices, for a little while

gift bearing a gift

thinking about john newlove
his alcoholic dad, his own child alcoholism
his leaving the prairie
and living on welfare
in vancouver
his eventual fame
his eventual sobriety
the way he is remembered
by his friends
by his fans
for his poetic hands
steady on the wheel of his works
while all else is disarray

depression and that thin line
of hope along the horizon
eyes damp with life's possibilities
while the siren calls from within, all
devastation embedded and encountered
luring the gaze inward
you can survive this, it's true
decisions have to be made
a body used to carve a mark
of self-pity on an alley wall, or
a taming of the sirens and
a few years left for balance

attention on the i & thou
a final assessment of
the reality you are
a gift bearing a gift bearing fruit
fruit so wild and sweet
poems so succulent
we are disarmed
eye-damp beauty

it's a blessing

with thanks to Chris Bose's Stone the Crow

i am reading his poetry
i become depressed with him
we hate the world mirror
become disarmed with despair
we fly together beyond starlight
investigate the spaces between
planets
between lovers' thighs, yes
we are hot and free and wistful
in our longings

we lay on the hotel bed, he says
somebody lied and i say
who the hell is that guy?
and why would you listen to him anyway?
survivor guilt is something we must survive
in order to experience, i tell him
it's a blessing

eventually, though, his farewells
and our potential farewells
come together
i fall out of his story
i return to you

i tell you
the world is on the brink of rain
i have only another
twenty pages
to read

conflict zone

—

capture

with thanks to Langston Hughes' "Catch"

he has something
i enjoy the taste of
open myself to him

hungry child suffused
with hopefulness the scents
of nourishment evoke

i cannot help myself
the way i am caught
is unexpected

so used to disappointment
subdued by blossoms fallen
invitations quickly revoked

all i can do
is lie quietly
watching

my eyes tracking
his every move

he takes my arms
he takes my legs

he strokes me softly
with wide, flat palms

a very big girl (languorous)

with thanks to Balayeurs du Desert,
Royal de Luxe & Cy Coleman

she wakes up
she rises from her chair
she has a shower, standing
under the spray
of the Sultan's elephant
channeling water despite
his skeletal ways

she strokes her braid

she blinks

she lifts her chin

small men peel off
her wet clothes, help
to dress her for the day
one foot, next foot, lift
gazing in wonder
she strolls into the morning
small smile touching her face

small men are touching
the back of her head
as she walks

she blinks

she lifts her chin

leading her on
clustering round behind her
so helpful, so helpful these men

she lifts a lollipop to her mouth
and she licks
slowly
she licks
slowly
and again
and again

she lifts her chin

lilliputian girls clamber
to sit astride her forearms
to ride

she gazes at them tenderly
with quiet wonder
she rocks them

when tired of this play
she turns away
small men lead her back
to her large, red chair

lower her gently

rest now
rest

into her dreams

I've learned to clip my wings
& soften my ways

unhinged

with thanks to Harold Rhenisch
& Robert Frost

a gate so long disused, along
the disappearing fenceline
holding a shape still, but unhinged
leaning against a post that is
itself
subject to the weather

how people die and farms
long untended, slowly return
with the help of gravity and grass
to a more subtle story about
making an attempt, launching a dream
rounding up hopes & dreams and herding them
corralled for the winter
or gently walking among the birch & poplar
then out to the back fields for pasture
when the season is warm

a gate so often opened and closed
secured by a twist of rope or wire
depending on the year and who
repaired it last, what they had on hand
while doing the dreamy work of fencing
a poet's job, for sure

and how people don't always die, sometimes
they simply sit down in the kitchen, drinking
too many pots of tea, or too many bottles
of their favoured hard liquor

there are so many ways that dreams can fail
and productive operations falter
and lines disappear into the tall grass
that once were vividly erected

a bloody man imposes his redness
on dinner: forgotten poem
with thanks to Sam Kaufman

a bloody man imposes his redness on dinner
beginning in the morning, hunted and proceeded
to slaughter, but forgetting

to ask permission first
to leave offerings
to give thanks

home again after, careful to wash
lifeblood from arms and hands and boots
missing the spray across his right ear entirely

proceeding to table, but forgetting
still

to ask permission first
to leave offerings
to give thanks

child eyes down behind lowered lids
lids thin as leaves in the forest sheltering birds
scent of blood and soap and dinner

intermingling

flushed cheeks all around
mouths
slowly chewing silence

Sah kee too win (elder's voice)

with thanks to Maria Campbell

When the shouting man emerges
over dinner, and a child flies up
the stairs to safety, the others
hunkered down in their chairs

when i rise up and work to divert
the flow of venom, the words
sah kee too win
are very far from my mind

later on, though, the words
drift back, like a butterfly
migration, and i remember
to pass them on to you

slowly, over time, my body
unclenches, her words
just continue writing love poems
roll through me, soothing

she tells us, the closest words to love
in Cree, *sah kee too win*
"holding each other close
as in kindness, warmth, and safety"

writers in exile (cordillera)

i would like to invite you
one day, to tell me your story.
here's mine:

i was in the trailer reading a novel
Vanity Fair, Where the Red Fern Grows, or
My Friend Flicka

one of those three, i read them all
in the hot grass & in the cool trailer
that summer

she came for a visit, slipped into
the trailer for privacy, started
moving her clothes all around

& looking at her own body
i kept reading
she drew my attention finally

look at this, & look at this
showing me the bruises
all over her back, front, both arms

she told me who did it, & when, & then
showed me the diamond ring
he'd given her, too.

i cling to this refuge
of ocean & sky, i hold tight
gather cordillera between anxious fingers

draw them up against me
like a grandmother quilt, to keep me
warm & safe from these   night visions

arriving as i did, on the coast, a refugee
with a broken heart & bruise minnows
swimming my neck.

she is riding

down through the suburban grey
streets dreamed by developers and
implemented for traffic floes

comes riding the turquoise green Grandmother
riding her mighty Sow
onto the battlefield

down along the highway of decay she rides
between the crack houses and on to piggy palace
where the spirits of the women are lifted

out of the horror, out of the muck, like
troubled teeth and bone fragments
their spirits gather and rise, and rise

all of our dead sisters lifted by those winged women
well-versed in the protocols of the battlefields
recognizing the existence of the battlefields, here

as along the highway of tears

shoulders back
open arms
open chested

the turquoise green grandmother breathes
along with each one of us still travelling
our inner city streets

our turns on the quiet highways
our love affairs gone wrong
our villages overrun

shoulders back
open arms
open chested

letting flow the sounds of the inside
the sounds of our voices calling out songs of sorrow
the sounds of our drums rising through time and through sky
the sounds of our warm bodies travelling swift
through the families
and through the forests

shoulders back
open arms
open chested

we accompany our sisters and brothers to the threshold
we hold them until they are fled, and then
we hold them more

we accompany our mothers and our fathers
we accompany our children, our friends, and o
the many strangers, the star gazers

we hold our dying persons long, dwell
inside memory

we lay each one to rest
slowly

shoulders back
open arms
open chested

tears coursing from the inside
across the outside and wetting
our multihued skins

the touch of a warm palm in passing
through hair on a child's head gently

the touch of lover to beloved
anywhere, at any time

the touch of Grandmother's warm palm
on the cheek of her adult offspring

or along the stiff hair on the Sow's back
she is riding

mourning song (a garden for you)

I wanted to tell you, I am sorry

I wanted to tell you, I would like to unmake the world for you
tear it down
tear it down
tear it down

and to make it, again, I would like to make it different for you
different
from the very root

I wanted to tell you, I would like to remake the world for you
I would like to remake the world with you in mind

I wanted to sing for you
I wanted to sing you a travelling song
a love song
a lullaby

I wanted to sing for you
a spirit-healing song that arrives
like a hand around the soul, soothing you
smoothing the way for you
nourishing

I want to build you a garden
plant a willow in your name
and watch it grow
below the trailing willow leaves
where the elders sit, the children play

not scattered by the power of forgetting
not scattered by the power of the parking lot
the condominium
the mall

not alone with it, each one carrying grief
like a shard in the heart

I want to remember you
by honouring you in this place

I want to remember you
by honouring your family
by honouring your friends
by honouring all of us who are touched
by undignified deaths

Let us make a home for our losses
a space for our memories
a home for our daughters

Let us remake the world in a small way
with this green garden

wild seeds

poppies have been the only thing
to thrive from the wild seeds
I scattered in February

so I will be getting some clover
and soil to be a blanket
for his bones

— Sandy Oliver, speaking of Ken
    Waldrone's gravesite/memorial

i.

we have love, we have grief
these two are guaranteed

we have birth
we have death

these, too, are promised

we have wild poppies on an island
nestled between a massive landbase

and a smaller landbase
and the sea

and although these
were not promised

this is what has grown
from the wild seed

ii.

in life, too
a blanket for our bones
woven of flesh and *qi*
is necessary

draped upon us, too
extending out from the frame
of our bones, the associations
we make

form a tent arising
above and around us
anchored to earth
our inescapable web

moving within with a deep sense
of purpose, organized around
love energies that flow and turn

well beyond the limits
of our mortal constraints
we are surrounded by portals

that appear and dissipate quickly
dropping gifts, or
taking back from us

what is most
cherished

iii.

we take one step at a time
through the portals

or beyond those glimpsed
but not meant for us

moving through the worlds
and shaping as we go

using all that we have to hand
the soil, the clover, the poppies

fallen comrades
lovers here & gone

recurrent flight
of geese overhead

rise of renewal
in a small green twist

underfoot

iv.

moonrise & set
rise & set

to be a blanket for his bones
is my heart's intention

though well i know
to love deeply will cost

to be blanketed by him
to keep the cold from gusting in

too far inside me
is my wish, my hungry desire

to be the soil for both
wild seed and clover

like a dreamscape
unfolding within

while overhead
moonrise & set

rise & set

an impressive array

our bodies are our selves, only
the feints of culture can obscure it
our bodies are the repositories of
every sense impression gathered
through a lifetime, or perhaps
many lifetimes, our bodies
are ourselves, rising up
from potential to real, our bodies
are the mark of our passing, our bodies
are the soft earth of self and the panoply
of thought streams and disruptions, the
culture-tangled nots and knots and naughts
our bodies are the ground of our beings, and
the playing fields of our minds, our bodies
are what we are good at, and unconscious of,
and what we are excited with, and thoughtful
through, our bodies arrived in the world
in order for us to drink beauty through every pore
and in order for us to express beauty
as an expression of the world itself, we are
a song the world enjoys singing to itself
we do not have our bodies
anymore than the world has us
a moment of self-possession passes
in the same way as does everything else

you need to tell me

I do, sometimes
I need to tell you
what is going on
bristling or building
like a wave inside of me
burgeoning like some
gestational entity, will
she leap from my forehead
or he from the side of his father's head
or a more traditional birthing expected
who can tell
what the next moment will bring
in a cross-fertilization process
that is pulling
at the core of
all
these tidy weavings —

challenge
and deep breathing

hoping to move the thick red branch
that proceeds from my centre
all across the world to you, invisible
placental placement
into a whole-bodied integrated flow
of beautiful weather

often fear arises
divisions may be too painful
the multiplications required, this
is a growth process, right? I ask
or spill theories that are so complex
wonder how we got here, really
just a simple arithmetical addition
and all the reverberations set off
by the simple constellation struck
one and one makes plenty
that's how it seems

when you tell me, though
you need to tell me
I feel anxiety coming through
& I move to soothe
drawing upon words and a flowing
fear conqueror
many-armed divinity with
lotus throne below
emanations and manifestations
sweeping the world clean
with hand brooms and two palms cupping
fresh water to replenish, small enough
to drink from, spacious enough
to hold an ocean
for you

a night for the lady (building bridges)

I always had a hankering for the
security of impossible dreams.
— Azar Nafisi

Sovann Macha
& Hanuman
diving for joy

began in opposition —
he charged with building
the bridge to Lanka

she charged with keeping
the waters open
running free

do you feel pursued?
not nearly enough!

they say the chase is
better than the catch, but i
disagree

the two
blend

world shapers

creation stories are lullabies
for grown-ups
they remind us of all the possible
ways & means
that worlds can be born
& humans come to be

tricksters & goddesses
fire & water
the one god, or all of the gods
working as a team

world-makers
world-shakers
world-breakers

there is no end to the doing & the undoing
of our creators
they have imagined us over & over & over
recreating us & recreating our world
on a whim

there is no end to us humans, either
we keep re-inventing the cosmos & fighting
one another's visions
with killing hands

we have our feast times
& our fast times
our celebrations & our long days & nights
of lament

yet we are not powerless
we reinvent, we shape and
reshape the world, every
single day

Desdemona (Durga)

he came at me in a fierce rage
i felt a small crack open in my
forehead, Kali
burst forth and struck him
a fierce blow
and he was felled
Kali continued
moving about the scene
devouring men high and low
and then
i said, *stop*
not the shaper
her eyes strayed toward Emilia
and again
i said, *stop*

with the place now cleared
but for the few left standing
Kali returned to slip inside
my head
i went to the cupboard
for rags and salt
i opened the closet
for the mop and bucket
started running cold water

no idea what Iago or Emilia
will do with themselves, but
a woman needs to keep her
attention on what she herself
needs to do: every good bloodbath
must be followed by a scrub and rinse,
a home is not a battlefield after all

a night for the lady (Shahrazad, storyteller)

Dunyázad, free the world

my slave my slave my sister
leading me on by clever means to
better things
in a house
built of many rooms that spill
each one contained, conjoined, connected
altogether across the mountainside
through the riverbottomlands
deep in the wooded places lost
in the grass, covered
in the daily falling snow, hidden
in the shifting sands
dislocated
dissociated
linked
all along the backs of hands and minds
the living and the dead together sing
rhapsody
monody
poetry
the whole world over
the whole world over
the whole world over, stories
spill and traverse the skins and permeate
our lives
the sound of the horses arriving at a run
the abrupt end of the scream that slashes
my heart
the rediscovered graves that now have sides
in human eyes

in human ears
in living minds
the concussions
of the bombs of the good

my slave my slave my sister
you who lead me on by
clever means
better things
await
a feast in the garden of our safekeeping
grandmother's ancient laughter at
the timing of this
thanksgiving
transmission
via peaceful means
of the glory of
of the glory of
of the glory of
our human being

my slave my slave my sister
i wrap the fabric round and round and round
i learn the arts
of careful draping
how to balance the water on my head
with the snake on the ground
how to balance
the fathers
of nuliajuk, kuan yin, ma tsu
with the guardians of the oceans of compassion
wherein you and i must swim and swim and swim
calling forth
the children of tomorrow
through these sacred slippery gateless gates
of self
the sweatdamp limbs

that part
allowing
this one into self
this one in a linked but separate migration
into the world
allowing
allowing
not captured not endangered not callously
overrun
not sundered by the sword of death
not split by the rule-bearing knuckles
of angry brothers
not slashed with impunity, kill this
and you kill the community
not slit and stitched with
well-meaning fingers
not
not
not
just
called forth
called forth, beckoned
called into the delicious warmth
of safe harbour
safe journey begins
by surging out toward that which
calls us in
gathering
the nourishing harvest
of all that we love

my slave my slave my sister
stories age and ages shift
slave becomes sister
counsellor becomes queen
the rise and the fall of the world-freer
dismissed

to diminutive roles
half-forgotten
discounted
o
world-freer
remember
remember where you come from
remember upon whose body
you sup
remember the sound of her
heartbeat
and the deep thrilling peace
at the sound
of her voice

my slave my slave my sister
mother of my heart
through all your many changes
there is none
more beautiful than you

longing:
five poems on
diverse matters

–

lawbreak

Such a tiny shift
from wrong knowing
to right seeing

I know I have power

When I ask myself
how do I exercise it here?
I feel hopeless

You've told me so often
when a person goes down that road
we can't stop them
we can't go with them to change
anything

We can only stay open to the chance
of their return
to the right path
to the red road

If you chose to rob the abstract
or the wealthy, I could perhaps go on
being your deep friend

Some laws are unfriendly
unnatural
some laws
beg to be broken

Break open the way things are
in the hope of finding
the way things

are meant to be

When you burn the medicines, and pray
when you call us together as brother, as sister

you evoke a wholesome power greater
than any one and one and one of us together
When you open your heart for healing
open your wide arms

to hold fast the walls of the world
so one of us can crumple

unleash ourselves, finally
and regroup and rise again

more wholesome
that is a great good

When you open your home
in privacy, though

when you use the circle
to impose silence?

In this
you disrespect
the medicines

In this way
you disrespect
the person
who has come to you for help
away from a lifetime of harm

You say you know
you have taken

right action in this

I said, at first I said
we will have to agree
to disagree

but I can't

I have to pull back
to the side of the road
you are on

return to my own
right knowing
right way
red road

You say
you saw a trap
you leapt into it

The trap
is a projection
of your own mind

Splayed across
human bodies
time after time

a perforated man

Artist at work, Seattle, 2000: "beauty from necessity"

the endless march of days
can be marked, and thus contained
on stiff paper: lines, vertical
lines, horizontal
paper, black or white
red or green

the negative space
between the lines so drawn
newborn rectangles

to each of these new beings
he assigns a name, one number
then cycling through some
time-honoured
patterning:

Dec	Jan	Feb	
S	M	T	W
22	23	24	25
31	1	2	

he affixes the marked card
to his bedroom wall
where it becomes a kind of compost
a gathering place

for slender, ultra-fine
short needle, ½ cc
disposable
syringes

in a popular song
we hear reference made
to *another man lost*
to the needle

playful, i ask
is that another
diabetes reference?

heroin
he responds, quietly
as if i didn't know already
as if i didn't
understand

each needle
with its sprightly orange cap
comes pre-marked
with thin black lines
and thick black numbers

5   10   15   20
all the way to 50
always the same numbers
always in the same sequence

we talk about
writing a screenplay
a romantic comedy

i want to include
a diabetic character
to whom nothing bad happens

he wonders, *why?*

he has a little book of days
that he keeps with his kit
why waste ritual?
why not gather souvenirs —

6:30	169	20N	4R	L
4:30	141	6N	2R	R
1:30	233	3N		L

6:30	128	20N	3R	L
4:30	60	6N	2R	R
10:30	80	2N		L

time   *6:30*

blood sugar level   *169*

how much of each kind of insulin*
20N   4R

which side of his human body
to press the needle in *L*

A retrospective:

over the years the ritual has changed
the cards and the books are new things
strategies of containment

the generation of a history
a track record
a paper trail

as a child, he used a glass needle
kept in the kitchen   disposable tips
insulin harvested from cattle and pigs
pee samples daily

---

* N = slow-acting insulin   R = fast-acting insulin

in his twenties still   he took a high dose
calibrated by a doctor not seen in years
based on his mother's   home cooking, by then
rarely eaten

in his forties, he used insulin
synthetically designed
by and for humans
the slow– and fast–acting together
in tiny increments

at fifty years of age
between the lancet and the needle
he now pokes small holes in himself
six times a day

hitch-hiking across Canada, 1981, my observations:

once a day
every day

he opens a small
silver-lined envelope
pulls out a folded paper cloth
drenched in alcohol

he swabs a small patch
of freckled skin
on an arm
or a leg

he pulls the white cap
from the plunger
pulls the orange hat
from the other end of the needle

then turns the insulin bottle
round and round and round
between careful fingers

he pulls the plunger back
an invisible measure
pierces the skin at the bottle's mouth
pushes air in

turning the bottle upside down
he holds the apparatus high
frowning
watching for bubbles

he pulls the tiny plunger just
exactly so, removes the bottle
flicks the needle, sometimes
does the whole job
over again
seeking perfection

finally
pops the metal tip
through his body's surface
expels
insulin

he spins the metal nib free
of the needle's body:
  a small sort of assertion of self
  a habit left over from earlier days
precaution against strangers
  re-using this needle
revenge
  on the tiny implement
  upon which his
life depends

newly immigrated to Canada, 2002, our basement apartment:

as the diabetic is
to the addict
so the nursing mother is
to the stripper

striving for balance
left side
right side
left side

if milk and insulin
are emulsive and arrive
in waves

this ritual alternation
forms the larger tidal pattern
of our days

> some say we choose in a spirit state
> each of our incarnations
>
> i wonder at his decision
> *i would like, at ten years of age*
> *to waste away*
> *to become liquid-obsessed*
> *to thirst wildly*
> *to pee frequently*
> *to stare hard at school clocks*
> *in desperation*

in a new country
in a new century

he shows a new doctor
his numbers, faithfully recorded

all about the doctor
excitement is stirring

he wants to discuss all
the awful possibilities

in the diabetic person
a kind of fatigue called

      new beginnings

Artist at work, Seattle, 2000:
"use once only and destroy"

he reaches up

and tapes the syringe
onto the newborn rectangle
on his bedroom wall

when the card is full
he mounts it on canvas
then buries it
in glue
in fabric
in paint

imaging, first
calendars of days
then his own face, his torso
taking a shot   with lace

items of clothing transform
into needle-strewn cityscapes
      friends' faces appear
on rippled carpets of needles

it is like a forest floor
in here

                if this
                weaving of words
                is a tapestry
                warp is the artist
                weft the diabetic
                transverse the man

four decades of diabetes elaborated
mapped and painted

a perforated man
quietly wielding and lacing

stitching his whole life
into the frame

the walls i remember

my father

my father is not just
the man with the guitar

he is the force that recreates
a whole wall of music
in the family home

at rest
they are guitar, guitar
ukelele, kook-a-lele*
tambourines, and a bongo drum

taken down
one by one or the
whole wall stripped
we are
really living

we believe in the happy chaos
of children and laughter
adults singing off-key and
really loud

alone with his guitar
he telegraphs the inside story
of the chaos that
overwhelmed that
living room

---

* kook-a-lele: four-stringed instrument with triangular base

the wall with the split
leather strap that looms
over our kitchen table
in later years

tightening stomachs through
mealtimes
applied against hands or backs
or childish bums

that wall holds also
a generous window
through which I watch
the seasons sing
across the land

the deluge of springtime
the slow conquering of green
the steady fade to yellow-browns until
in a guitar season
strings of silver frost call forth
the silence
of winter

long after the strap
is taken down
in the core of our house
remains his abiding gift, his
invitation

a guitar, a guitar, a banjo
a bow and fiddle together

hung upon the wall beside
portraits of his children

on apron flapping

I love an old story. Old stories
are the food I eat and
the water I drink. Old stories
are the furniture
my children and I
rest upon.

With old stories
we stitch together
the clothing we wear
and with old stories
we erect the shelter that we need
in times of big weather.

Old stories come to me
in many ways.

Most of the old stories
that I know
come from foreign lands
and describe foreign
landscapes. What
can I do?

Bible stories, Kali-Durga
stories, European
nursery rhymes:

I feel embarrassed
standing at the front of a room
leaning against old pre-Iraqi prayers
to describe the joy of a young prairie woman
feeling sexual. Why

must I go back thousands of years
to find a traditional word
to celebrate
something so human?

I have borrowed
aunties and grandmas
from many communities.
They have told me healing tales
and taught me songs
that allowed me to weep hard
and after the flow of great tears
to move on
holding my head up
grasping the earth
and letting it go again
with every step I take
feeling trust.

It's okay.
I'm okay.

But no one has told me, Joanne,
take this story with you
tell this to the world.

Everyone has told me, Joanne,
go out in the world
and tell *your* stories.

And so I have told my stories
of travelling with a man who,
in order to win an argument
strangled me into unconsciousness:

I have told my old stories
of being trapped in root cellars,

of being hungry,
of petty theft, and all of its consequences
of striking my son:
of the rages
that have stormed across
the many landscapes
of my life:

the prairie landscapes
the great lakes landscapes
all across the lower mainland
with the slap of the sea
sounding
in my ears.

I have told my stories
of dipping in mysteries —
the death of my beloved
grandmother —
the times I have held people
inside my belly
then felt them pull away
tumbling into a landscape
we call the earth and
we call home —

I feel embarrassed now
to have been so very angry
with my ancestors.
Like me, they were just
trying to get along.

The oldest story that I know
that has been passed down
through the generations of women
in my family

that was given to me
from my grandmother's mouth
happened in France, or possibly
in Belgium.

The men had been away a long time
and whether they were defending
their own boundaries
or conducting yet another campaign
against indigenous people somewhere
my grandma didn't say.

The women were overjoyed
and somewhat afraid
at the return of the men

come away!
come away!

The women called one another
from their chores
to rush down to line the roads
along which the men
were walking home.

The women, as was the fashion
in that time and place
expressed the intensity of their feeling
by grasping the edges of their aprons
and flapping them.
It must have been a fine sight
and a longed-for vision
to the war-stricken and love-
starved eyes
of the men, like snow geese
lifting off all together
and resettling

on the marsh

all that material like wings
flapping

flapping the enthusiasm
of a community
coming together again
saying hello to itself

saying
I love you
saying
I missed you.

The fine art
of apron-flapping
is not one that has come down
to me directly
these many generations
these many many miles
i cannot teach
this to my daughter
although, should we choose to,
we could re-imagine it.

Although there are only
the two of us
we could stand
at the top of the stairs
and flap aprons
at the boys
coming home from school
and at the men, coming home from work
one at seven in the morning
and another at five in the evening.

It sounds like fun, actually
we might try that.

But, to get back to
the old story
to finish telling the oldest
story that I know
that has come down to me
through my maternal line
that first happened in France
or maybe in Belgium
a long long time ago to a woman
of my ancestral line

told from woman to girl
down through a couple of centuries
and across these many changes
and these many, many miles:

Upon the vigorous, hearty flapping
of her apron
it was revealed
that under her apron
her dress had been damaged
and was now patched.

What
am I to make
of this story?

Why was this tale
of embarrassment
so very important
that generation after generation
after generation
we have been compelled

to remember this story
to tell this story to one another

forgetting all the stories
of a young woman's sexual waking
of a bride's joy in grasping
her husband hard between her thighs
of a mother burgeoning
and then birthing
and then breastfeeding her beautiful,
powerful, vulnerable young

forgetting our love of
ourselves, our work, our communities
of our landscapes
of our journeys
of our spiritual
worlds.

We have chosen to remember
a time when we were caught
unprepared
an occasion upon which, dressing
to do chores
an unexpected event revealed to all
the patch upon our dress

and how somehow
having the patch pointed out to us, perhaps
it made us feel
unacceptable
not a part of things
foolish
ashamed.

On behalf of the many generations
of the women in my family
and of the men,
all the way back in time
from our scattered and diverse
places of origin
places of marriage
places of childbirth
places of death and of burial:

We are sorry
to disturb you
by participating.

We are sorry
for revealing
over and over again
with every flap of the apron
the damages suffered
the patches and the scars
and the ongoing need
for healing
and for reparation.

We are sorry
if we make you uncomfortable
and we are
nevertheless
very happy to see you
and very, very happy to be here.

We are eager to share story
and to share song with you
to share food with you
and shelter
to share community

and even, to marry
all of you
apparently
patches and all.

My sons and their fathers
myself and my daughter
we make use of old stories to warm
the cold nights
to sing in
the new day
the new season
the ever-hatching new world

and to build our
new stories upon
in the old way.

I, Joanne Arnott, born on the banks
of the Assiniboine River
having lived, loved, raged and cried
beside many rivers
and now
living on a stone in the mouth
of the Fraser River:
I have now shared with you
the oldest story
that has come down to me
through my family
so far:

thank you
for listening.

land in place: mapping the grandmother

inspired by Christi Belcourt's Mapping Routes of Ontario

It is not just white people who have
Métis grandmothers

It is not just black people who have
Métis grandmothers

It is not just yellow people who have
Métis grandmothers

It is not just red people who have
Métis grandmothers

From all the directions
the grandmothers come

intermingling languages, stories, blood
braiding a river of human

inter-relations
interlocutions

bawdy songs and body songs and
storied landscapes

Think of the old communities, and our ties
to the lands of our old stories

our minds returning our selves to mother tongues,
    to native tongues
re-wrapping our bodies around these new-old sounds

new-old syllables
new-old rhythms

new-old sensibilities & loves
redrawing the maps, and pulling

fresh wisdom from the old music
we formed around

inside the dancing vessels of
our mothers, vital daughters of

our
grandmothers

Still, so often it comes, the time returns
when we have to pack our things and move again

every single time we move, some thing
is left behind

a ladle
a small cup

an obstinate person
a story, cherished much

We have our desperate moments, too
when memory of all that is lost rises full

casting long shadows across the moon-tinted & starlit
landscape

and so the sorrow of the long good-bye
becomes a part of our heritage

the unspoken, unwilling partings
the sudden deaths, the midnight moves,
the lost children
sighing in our dreams
the silent elder

look around you
look around you, now, and know this

There are Métis Grandmothers standing
all around you

some rising to cusp the horizon
some falling to blanket the earth

some growing between blades of grass
some winging across a concrete-shackled homeland, still

very much alive
still singing

experiment

a whisper song

shh shh my darling *shh shh*
shh shh my darling *shh shh*
all will come out right
all will come out right

shh shh my darling *shh shh*
shh shh my darling *shh shh*
all will come out right
all will come out right

shh shh my darling *shh shh*
shh shh my darling *shh shh*
i will hold you tight
i will hold you tight
i will hold you tight
shh shh

knotwork tapestry

i dream that we follow a knotted string
all the way back to our deepest selves

holding the vision, steadily working
the small weave with delicacy

accumulation of unattended details, loose threads
lack of conclusion on every front may undo

picking up more & more beginnings
new colours and shapes forming

under my hands
mid-weave is an uncertain place

mid-weave is an uncertain place
under my hands

new colours and shapes forming
picking up more & more beginnings

lack of conclusion on every front may undo
accumulation of unattended details, loose threads

the small weave with delicacy
holding the vision, steadily working

all the way back to our deepest selves
i dream that we follow a knotted string

a really good lament

"'tis i'll be there
in sunshine or in shadow"
— Frederick Weatherly, "Danny Boy"

i am aware of my mortality
i try to have a good time, despite
my hyper-vigilant responses

like a newborn babe, not used
to all the usual things
of this earth

not used to it yet

having been handed the brush
& having brushed death til it gleamed
i find it hard to set it down again

i'm afraid i don't know how

it's easy, now, not to be
completely enchanted
by the deep gloss, the deep thick coat of it

no desire to tangle my fingers there
no desire to bury my face in it

i have given birth six times since then
i have had too much celebration
to be attracted to that anymore

i want to tangle my fingers in sweetgrass
i want to bury my face on your chest, just there
i want you to kiss me, let me taste that instead

i want to put the brush down
free my hands entirely
take up other implements

a scale of souls, perhaps
a drum for the women
a sword of justice

a simple cooking pot
a single flower
a willow branch

i want to put the brush down, free
my two hands for embracing
small children

for embracing you
if you will be embraced by me
i don't yet understand

one of the beautiful things that i know
is the feeling of a really good lament
in full flow

a lament is a mark of the shapes of our lives
the power of our loving attachments
& giving tongue to these

feels good
feels true
feels free

i would like to be
life's champion
not death's handmaiden

i would like to have the longevity
of my grandmothers
& fly free

disturbances in the field

Salmon people fomented revenge and tied DFO to a dark poem.
— Michael Blackstock, "Wyget and the Fisheries Biologist"

eagle patrols the suburb in long, slow, silent circles
helicopter bisects the sky, ear-catching

there are disturbances in the field, blind & deaf
i can still feel them

when it is i who am disturbed
i can plumb the depths, pull up stories in my net

when it is you who are disturbed
i am tied to a dark poem, only, waiting

imagination turns to terrible invention
intellect tries to remain measured, despite all

a part of you has smiled
at a part of me

i wish the visceral confidence would rise
up from the seabed of wordless self

inhabit my full consciousness
dependent upon the words that are now lost

to the cutting room floor
the mice in your room know your mind

better than i do

salmon people have tied DFO*
to a dark poem, too

hoping for a transformation
in the world to follow

i hold the pebble in my mouth
and i shall never spit it out

until i stand on a gravel bank somewhere
with you

eagle feast on salmon
even in the suburbs

time-management isn't an issue
among the mice

helicopter carries DFO
high above all, a liberation

a dark poem holds
its own radiance

---

* DFO — Department of Fisheries and Oceans

be true

"in thinges touching conscience, euery true and good subject
is more bounde to haue respect to his saide conscience
and to his soule than to any other thing in all the world beside. "
— Thomas More

i.

my son hands me the program from the recent production
of *A Man for All Seasons*
when i was just his age, i pored over that text, i loved this play

i look at it now, from many angles
presented by the Midnight Theatre Collective, i see
Shanti Counselling has the back cover, asking

Do you have a personal or relationship problem?
Would you benefit from talking to a professional?
perhaps i have, i think, & no, i'll handle this

he hasn't brought me the play itself, but i do some research
o thomas MORE
o robert BOLT

o my young self:
what have they to say to me?
the morality of divorce, even with

the motive of further begatting
well behind me
is the lesser theme, i think

ii.

i have always loved the soliloquy on silence
the careful measures of wrong & right
the importance of being true

while you are away
i sit quietly
i think of these things

the meanings of silence
what all the words and all of the silences mean
taken together

because it is in the nature of the way we have
befriended one another, that i see things about you
that are not about me, & i find that these delight

at the same time, circumstantially & without a marching band
i have revealed almost all of my injuries to you
& you have received them, & we carry on

the very elements of me so injured
have found freedom in your silence
the call for you arises in the voice of the once-injured girl

even more loudly than
the hungry woman's
hunting growl

the very parts of me who sat in the courtroom & listened
the very parts of me who watched her hands lose power, unable
now that she has finally realized that she must fight for her life

to do so

watching my hands drop back toward me
feeling my bladder & bowels release
so deep, this surrender

so dangerous for me

the very one who taught me vigilance
the very one who showed me the consequence
of placing my self in a stranger's hands

she is the one who so optimistically interprets your silence
she swears you and your attachment to the world
is exactly, precisely, perfectly: medicine for me

wait

with thanks to Anna Marie Sewell

i. *earthquake*

preponderantly slow
the earth
is in motion

the layers of the solid
drift along the molten
like leaves
on a river

from far below
heat
melts the hardened

exploratory fingers rise
forging new pathways
some abandoned soon
others pursued to make

new realities

the leaves on the river
gather together then swirl apart
and move along forever

plunged to the depth
rolled in stones at the riverbottom
become one with the mud
or pushed hard against the edges

of the waterway

layers of solid earth, too
meet, part, meet again
some pull away, slow decay

others climb over themselves
with enthusiasm
new cordillera are forming
every single day

when the earth pushes up
against itself like this
slips and sudden moves
shudder our world

to the quick
all of us jump up
or cower down, or both

when the earth
shakes her self awake

we are all propelled to live
by instinct

ii. *tidal wave*

early signs are noted
by the human animal

connected to
all our relations

a sense of difference
a sense of a quality of change

in the feel and taste of things
in the sounds of the morning

in the nuance base

our bodies are more
responsive to the meaning

of the signs
than intellect is

intellect scrambles
to interpret

often fails
often flails

intellect is always
the first victim

of the inrushing wall
of water

swamped & shocked
it rides along

helpless
while the human animal

does everything within
our power

to surf the wall of change
to survive the journey

   iii. *ocean*

my dear, each of us
has to hand
an ocean

our oceans are known
by different
names

our oceans are said to be
very far
apart

but we know
you know, and
i know, there is only one

ocean

and this ocean
can be slipped into
can be leapt into

can pull us and drag us
of its own volition
boldly inside of itself

from many
many different
shores

the whole world over

iv. *wait*

natural pauses occur
in the shape
of everything

hold

warmth of face untouched and laughing
eyes and loving smile
who would cook for me
who would regale me with thoughts and stories
the music of his voice and the flow of life
from his vibrant core
all of his stories summarize thus —
the world is wondrous
we are all doomed
don't give up

she plucks the strands of her web
a musical hum begins
her world is delicious
smiles arise and shine across
all her relations

love love love
is shining through
spilling sorrow for the world
in its wake

winter visit

the spring birds chuckle in the trees
the world rainwashed and shining
the lady on the mountain is calling
for snow
showing my hand to my love
i feel, first gladness, then sorrow

crow brushed my hair in flight
startled from a lowhanging branch
turning in midair to take a look
at me
showing my hand to my love
i feel, first gladness, then sorrow

a journey is planned for next week
anticipation turns to dread
trepidation slows my hand across
the page
showing my hand to my love
i feel, first gladness, then regret

dissolute poem (aurora)

i.

walking from the sleepbound house
through dew and
through the dawn's light

she came upon a percheron
massive in the tall grass
quietly monumental

his tail a cascade of hair
switching gently against
the round full beauty of his rump

ii.

rumpled, she walked forth
beyond the screen of poplar
approaching the naked horse

mindful of the day's work ahead
the weight of it, caught by desire
filling her

illuminated morning moments
her feet a *shooshoo* through the grass

iii.

i am stroking your morning hide
feel your limbs stirring softly
under my hand

your scent fills me
heat encompassing me
i am climbing across you

like a goddess taking a mountain
flesh to flesh
flesh to flesh

iv.

feeling the weight of her hands
i am alive to her, i want
to
    catch her in my hair
absorb her through the pores
of my skin
hide her within

i want to
shake her off
toss her into the grass
clasp her in two hooved arms

i want to plunge inside
and find a new home
in her

v.

dissolutions progress
sun strengthens, dew
both absorbed and burnt away

girl and woman
horse and woman
woman and man

grass, poplar, house, land
everything

Oed's dream

i. *James Clerk Maxwell Redux*

conceive of a being whose faculties
are so sharpened

he can follow every molecule
in its course

such a being!

attributes essentially as finite
as our own

able to do
what is impossible to us

suppose a vessel divided —

division in which there is —

being who can see —

only the swifter molecules to pass
only the slower molecules to pass

thus
without expenditure of work

raise the temperature

ii. *Oed to a Large Tuna in the Market (after Neruda)*

once
sappy as a sprung fir
in the green turmoil

once seed
to sea-quake
tidal wave, now

in the whole market
the only shape left
with purpose or direction

my regular spot

for Jamie Reid, with thanks to Sandra Stephenson

at this time of year
when voles, moles and mice and shrews
make their way indoors
the black water backs into the basement
surprising us with all that was withheld, for years
just on the brink of us
just out of sight

the vice of autumn, the views too
veer from clay earth, root cellars
antiquated aqueducts and sewage pipes
on mountainsides
to the clean wet world without
a long look and a longer breath, north
from the high southern porch

a lingering walk in the garden
soaked in memories and lightly scented
with contentment
a warm and central person
free of the radiant lines of relatedness
and all of the consequences of relatedness
for one moment, catching sight

of crow and cloud and poetry
amidst a new season of damp and
colourful leaves

i placed my hand on Lenin's cheek

with thanks to the Gao Brothers

i placed my hand on Lenin's cheek this evening
his head a full metallic glimmer in the moonlight

Mao with a long balancing rod in hand, stood still
upon his crown

i stepped back, glanced over my shoulder
to the high placed moon

i placed my hand on Lenin's cheek this evening
& thought of you

"blue grouse wakens stars for us"

with thanks to Fred Wah

i.

on a sandy sideroad, flanked by birch-poplar-grasses-aspen
in the shade of them, on a hot sun day

the mother and her many chicks straggle
out of the wild world

into the sunlit road
tumble play hophop

i watch as they go about their lives
unperturbed by my city-scent small shade

ii.

"Do not cry havoc, where you should but hunt
with modest warrant." Lest the craving for sanctum
inadvertently unleash
the wild torrent

Glaciers in concert tempestuously transform
throwing themselves away in a heat
while old forms
scrape and tumble, strange new landscapes self-create

O vertigo
this river didn't flow by here
when i was a girl

floruit

the girl with the jack-o'-lantern smile

see sea see sea
of humanity we
fail to distinguish
froth flow
feelings elide slide mingling

slow as the dawn
just that swift
sliding in under to breach and spout
slapping down with the clatter of a whale

i move apart
i flow between
i circle back

permeable envelope
continuous with
all that is contained

selfsame

in the sea of grass
winter calling
a breath of frost
to kiss upon the blades
throwing thistle
into high relief
not a straightline
visual quivers

in the sea of earth
root cellar girls swim
away from all that was delivered
though never promised
away from all that was promised
and never given
sliding past the ancestors
furious breaststrokes
grabbing our roots in our teeth
gliding away

in the sea of heaven
the constellations gleam and dim

in the sea of autumn
the girl with the jack-o-lantern smile
lit from within

for what is involved

*"For what is involved is undertaking the creation
of the world one has chosen to inhabit."*

— Mircea Eliade

slow saturnian stroll across
the sunrise point, my face
reflecting the dew
i am sure, i am all the time sure
that what i do is correct, and
in a deep way, mistaken

contrary dancing requires
this pull against the stream
the community makes space for
the one so called upon to spin
in opposition to the ordinary ways
of doing things

not extraordinary
subordinary
a small and minor note
subordinate to the needs of the sacred
puppet to the deeper pull between
planets & birds

dream portal

my daughter tells me
that i dreamt i was turned into mush
& that the mermaids saved me

i have no memory of this
but do not argue, we are all
dreaming one another anyway

there is no start or finish to it
the dream economy will thrive
in all kinds of weather

we pass our dreams back & forth
between the generations
as lateral gifts

as cross-cultural contagions
what does the dream contain?
what does the story hold?

when i assert, on another day
that i do remember
my life as a mermaid

my son affirms, *it's true*
ma remembers all of her
crazy adventures

floruit

Floruit: L., fl., the time of flourishing
Fruit: O.Fr., harvest, virtuous action

the light bulb and my coat together have made
a lovely lingam on the floor beside
the table's shade

the voice of the sleeve
sings of hidden matters

south of the walls of the north

for Angye & Azalea Gaona

this small room and the child i swore to make a safe and
excellent world for, just for you, just for you and the me
that is touched and touched and touched by your small
saunterings

the big world mounting around us high and high as far as
eye can see, well beyond that, feel the weight of the waves
coming in to pummel this beach, my belly, this beach, my
this

belly of home, all across the walls of the house the world
impends, steadily pressing, we have our guns they whisper
we have our armies, dear, we brought them for you, smell
taste

my police forces, my careless cocktails of whose words
will and whose will not, whose voice will and whose will
not, whose blood will and whose will not, whose girl are
you?

come ride with me in my wonderful *machina*. i have eaten
bigger trees than you and nourished larger pockets than
you will ever be. sleep with me and i can make all of this
o

putting our lives on the line to make a better world here
now turning my womb inside out to show here how now
this exposé o release me dammit, if i can just rest i can
think

beyond the machinery of state that has got us patiently
waiting for more of the same to the good, or more of the

same to the treacherous side of creation. breathe slow and
deep

bodily boldly okay. i can make a girl a man a poem a home
i can taste wind and the sea flowing over all of the impending
to tell me and by virtue of telling me telling you but just
listen

draw on the well like i told you, here, all you have learned
of the world you can use to make a new one a green and a
blue one with all the autumn colours and the deep surprising
nature

of the flowers. you can make the excellent sea the restful
day you can make or house a point and for the pleasure of
the ancestors and in the vindication of all of the lost i have
found

i will do this, just and joyous. but for now try to sleep and if
i can make a make or a life i will if i can i will i told you, here
draw listen sing soon wait wait wait o darling, despite the fire
arms

leaning up against the walls of the house, know the just men are
after all just men, and can be persuaded and yet may succumb.
i will keep synthesizing danger and truth and making beauty for
you

while others will carry our names, and do the same for me too.
we are a safe well of creation and the well of danger no deeper
than us. the ancestors, the new words, the poets, the old words
the wrong roads

and the right relationships unfurling on a cloudy day. and i know
the sun's light. i know the clarity. i can find my words and the will
to finish what was started and to strengthen what was weakened
that day.

BACKGROUNDS

The title for this collection I found on a stroll down Broadway, in Vancouver: "A Night for the Lady" was the name of a benefit gathering honouring Aung San Suu Kyi, iconic political person of Burma/Myanmar. Somehow the balance of honouring and political activity spoke to me strongly, evocative of both the Divine Lady (or Ladies) of my Roman Catholic youth, and the regional ways of speaking that I am at home in, a more casual and often affectionate use of the term.

I had the honour of working with Maria Campbell and The Aunties Collective in organizing and experiencing Mothers Journey, a week-long master-class retreat with Maria and a dozen other indigenous mother-writers of Canada. "Sah kee too win (elder's voice)" quotes Maria Campbell, a timely intervention and good-hearted advice. "a very big girl (languorous)" contains a ten-word quotation from a song originally written by Cy Coleman, and was written in response to an excellent short video/YouTube creation featuring the named performers and puppeteers. "a bloody man imposes his redness on dinner" was inspired by a line by Sam Kaufman (the title).

The Azar Nafisi quote in "a night for the lady" occurred in her powerful book, *Reading Lolita in Tehran*. The oral stories best known in the West as *1001 Arabian Nights* continue to be told. The frame story exploring aspects of gender violence and storytelling empowerment are the backdrop to this poem. They are infused with my intimate contents. My choice to use older or less familiar versions of the names of the "City Freer" and the "World Freer" (that is, the two core women of the frame story) was intended to assist in connecting with the meanings of the names, words and deities (just as elsewhere I chose to write "pre-Iraqi prayers" instead of "Sumerian").

Thanks to Rachel Quitsualik for her several essays on the being who became the base for the English-evoked deity, "Sedna." "land in place" was inspired by both an art show and a presentation of her research by Christi Belcourt ("Off the Map" and "Great Métis of My Time," Urban Shaman Gallery). "a really good lament" quotes the words of a song by Frederick Weatherly (nine words). "be true" contains a quote by Thomas More, spoken at his trial in England. "disturbances in the field" contains a quote from a story by Michael D. Blackstock. "wait" was composed in response to a series of random words assigned by Anna Marie Sewell, on our poetry e-group.

Several images and lines in "my regular place" were poached from a letter by Sandra Stephenson to Jamie Reid, which I then morphed into a freestanding poem/summary/tribute. "i placed my hand on Lenin's cheek" was inspired by some very controversial public art presented in the city of Richmond by the Gao Brothers of Beijing ("Mao balancing on Lenin's head"). "blue grouse wakens stars for us" is composed of two poems written in response to two poems by Fred Wah: "the blue grouse wakens stars for us" is a line in his work "poem-pictograph 33"; the second poetry aspect responds to his poem "Havoc Nation."

"south of the walls of the north" was inspired by Colombian poet, student, journalist, all-around artist and single mom, Angye Gaona, who for a time lived under house arrest with her small daughter, in a home variously described as "a room" and "a very small apartment." This poem was translated into Spanish by Susana Wald, and variously published (as consciousness-raiser and as fundraiser) in support of Ms. Gaona and her family.

ABOUT THE AUTHOR

Joanne Arnott is a Métis/mixed-blood writer and arts activist living in Salish territories, based on an island in the mouth of the Sto:lo River (Richmond, BC). She has lived in the lower mainland for thirty-five of her fifty-two years. Mother to five sons and one daughter, all born at home, she is poet, essayist, activist, mentor and blogger. A founding member of *Aboriginal Writers Collective West Coast*, Joanne facilitated Unlearning Racism workshops for many years, and continues to apply peer counselling and storytelling strategies in her work in the literary arts. She has volunteered with The Writers Union of Canada (National Council 2009–2010), and currently is a member of the Author's Advisory Group of The Writers Trust of Canada. She has published seven books, all well-reviewed, with *Wiles of Girlhood* (Press Gang, 1991) winning the Gerald Lampert Award.

ABOUT THE COVER ARTIST

Aaron Paquette is one of Canada's premier First Nations artists, known for his bright colours, strong lines, and for sharing new ways of looking at age-old experiences and beliefs. Based in Edmonton, Alberta, Aaron has been creating art for the past twenty years. He apprenticed and has become both a cathedral stained-glass artist and a goldsmith, influences of which can be seen in the line and structure of his paintings — displayed in various galleries throughout the country. Find out more about this artist, beloved teacher and gifted blogger on his website, http://www.aaronpaquette.net